Five of Us!

By Susan Yuen

Target Skill Consonant Blends

Scott Foresman
is an imprint of

One spins.

She spins and spins.

Two slid.

They slid fast.

Three are on top.

Three can drop and land.

Four hid.

Four hid in the sand.

Five ran.

They spot Mom.

Five are hot.

They plop and flop.

One, two, three, four, five.